The CONWY VALLEY
and its long history

Michael Senior

Printed and published in Wales by Gwasg Carreg Gwalch,
12 Iard yr Orsaf, Llanrwst, Dyffryn Conwy, LL26 0EH.
☎ *(01492) 642031* 🖷 *(01492) 641502*
e-mail: books@carreg-gwalch.co.uk
website: www.carreg-gwalch.co.uk

ISBN: 0-86381-035-7

BEFORE HISTORY

EVERY season the sandbanks of the Conwy river shift a little in their shape and size, in turn changing the river's channel. Indeed every tide the sand of the lower river is slightly redisposed. But the underlying form of the river bed has remained remarkably constant throughout thousands of years, and so therefore has the broad pattern of these surface features.

The long history of the Conwy Valley takes much the same form of continuous, noticeable surface change within a basic structure of quite remarkable constancy. It has been radically disturbed by only a few traumatic events, one of the first of which was the coming of man.

Mankind's effects on the valley have been at work for at least four thousand years. It is mainly his doings and his works which we shall be looking at in this booklet, though the effects of nature too continue to play a part in what has become, in the end, a co-operating partnership. But the valley had been forming itself without our help for some millions or years before the first human colonists discovered it.

Until the glaciers of the ice ages carved the hills into their present moulded forms, it is thought that the mountains of Snowdonia would have consisted of one vast and even dome. The drainage channels flowing from this would in the course of time find their routes along rock-faults, and one such line developed into what is now the Conwy Valley.

That was perhaps some fifty million years ago. Talking in terms of such numbers becomes meaningless in the tiny time-scale of human lives. But during the last few million years an effect took place which we can still quite clearly see, when the whole of this part of the world several times became entirely covered with ice.

As the ice formed itself in the uplands into glaciers, these crawled towards the natural channel of the Conwy Valley which then led them to the sea. In doing so they smoothed out the courses of subsidiary valleys and straightened some of the main valley's curves. But the Conwy is a river valley which was used by glaciers, rather than made by them, and it does not bear the long straight U-shaped form characteristic of many of Snowdonia's true glacial valleys.

As the glaciers melted, the tops of them continued for some time to eat back into the hillsides until they formed hollows, accentuated by a lip of deposited boulders, in the end trapping a lake in the bowl between eroded cliff and built-up lip. In this way there came about those features of the terrain so frequent in this part of Snowdonia, for which the Welsh word 'cwm' has now become the general technical term.

1 Standing stone above Ro Wen.

2 Cwm Dulyn

3 The two stones beside
the Roman road at Bwlch-y-ddeufaen.

4 Maen-y-Bardd cromlech.

The most distinctive of these cwms face north and east, where the ice lingered longest, and may be seen in the uplands above the valley at Llyn Dulyn and Llyn Melynllyn (Ordance Survey grid reference 700667 and 701657). These are expeditions for the walker, but the more accessible lake valleys of Crafnant, Geirionydd and Cowlyd, though much larger, were all made in the same way.

The pattern of vegetation in the valley during the post-glacial period, which takes us into observable times, has varied slightly with changes in climate which controlled the height of the line at which trees would grow on the upland slopes, and this in turn was what originally decided where the first human settlements would occur. At those times when the tree line was highest the weather would of course have been milder, so that occupation of the hills was practicable at much greater heights then than it is today. The deep peat deposits at 2750 feet above sea level on the plateau above Cwm Eigiau, for instance, (693659), show quite clearly that for much of the period of prehistory almost the whole of the area we are considering would have been covered by thick undergrowth and, lower down, dense forest. It was for this reason that the very early settlements tended to take place not here in the valley but on coastal promontories where the salt air discouraged the growth of trees.

Towards the end of the period we know as the late Stone Age, and into that of the early Bronze Age, during the third millennium B.C., the climate became cooler and drier. It is from this time on that the works of man became apparent in the Conwy Valley.

We are lucky to have, in fact, some superb examples of the oldest of all man-made structures in Britain, the megalithic chamber tombs. A very fine and well-preserved one, known as Maen-y-Bardd, *the Bard's Stone,* stands beside the Roman road above Ro Wen. (740718). Though not as large as some elsewhere, it possesses such firm proportions and such a lofty stance on the mountain's flank that it bears an unmatched air of nobility. Being in very much its original state it also illustrates the principles of construction of these neolithic burial chambers, by which a large capstone is poised on four or five uprights.

The tombs were originally covered over with a mound of earth and small stones, though it is not certain that the mound at Maen-y-Bardd was ever completed. A more elaborate example of a chamber tomb in this area, in which the mound is in place, occurs at Capel Garmon, above the eastern valley slope (819543). Here one can see a tomb consisting of not one but three linked chambers, a passage leading into them, and a long oblong concealing mound. Once again a superb outlook over largely unchanged landscape gives

5 Capel Garmon cromlech.

6 Cromlech near Glan Conwy

7 Bronze Age burial cairn near the Roman road at Bwlch-y-ddeufaen known as Barclodiad-y-Gawres.

a sense of timelessness. From both sites the limit of the present treeline indicates the level below which, for these late-Stone-Age builders, the valley would have effectively uninhabitable.

Although the tomb at Capel Garmon has been excavated, its treatment over the intervening ages had destroyed most of its original remains, and only small pieces of bone and pottery were found. These however are sufficient to date it about 2500 B.C., which is consistent with similar tombs elsewhere, and to indicate that its use continued from neolithic into Bronze Age times.

The chances against anything surviving so long, through such great stretches of ignorance and change, indicate that since in this valley alone there are four remaining examples of the type, there must at one time have been very many more. The other Conwy Valley specimens, though by no means as fine or as well-preserved as Maen-y-Bardd and Capel Garmon, are down near the river at Glan Conwy (794748), where a massive capstone now lies partly fallen from its supports, and near to Capel Garmon at Nebo (844567). This however, known as Maen Pebyll, is in poor condition; compared to the remarkable state of preservation of Capel Garmon it is a rather unimpressive ruin. The site is fine, however, in upland air overlooking an extensive rolling view, at the edge of moorland. Alone among all the valley's prehistoric monuments, the Glan Conwy tomb contradicts the principle that life at this time took place only at high levels, and some valley clearance must therefore already have begun.

The arrival of new people in the area is marked, for us, mainly by their introduction of new ways of burying the dead. From about 2000 B.C. the area was penetrated by people of a more complex culture, that of the Bronze Age. We do not have any certain remains of their dwellings, though some of the hut circles which continued to be in use right through Roman times may have originated at this period. We do have a number of stone cairns containing burial cists, the form which we know these people adopted for burial.

Some of these, remarkably, occur at a great height. One is on the summit of Carnedd Llywelyn itself, at 3485 feet the highest in this range, and indeed the highest mountain in England and Wales after the two main peaks of Snowdon. Another lies on the neighbouring summit of Foel Grach. For those who are not mountaineers the easiest to view lies not far from Maen-y-Bardd, where the Roman road runs through a natural pass known as Bwlch-y-ddeufaen, '*the Pass of the Two Stones*'(716716). The standing stones from which the pass gets its name may be seen a little further on, and are good examples of many such unexplained upright pillars in this area. They are similar in shape and position to the stone circles elsewhere, and may well belong to this early Bronze Age period.

BEFORE HISTORY

The cairn below the Roman road at Bwlch-y-ddeufaen is known as Barclodiad-y-Gawres, *'the giantess's apronful'*, the explanation of which curious title gives us a glimpse of how people traditionally viewed these very remote areas of the past.

A giant and a giantess were on their way through this pass in the hills, planning to build a house for themselves on the island of Anglesey. He was carrying two massive stones for the doorway, she had her apron full of smaller stones for the walls. As they reached this point they met a shoe-mender coming the other way. In the manner of itinerant medieval workmen he carried round his neck a long string of old shoes which he was going to mend. The giant asked him how far it was to Anglesey. Perhaps having something against giants, he indicated the shoes: 'I have worn out all these shoes on the way from there.' In simple-minded despair, the giant threw down his two stones, the giantess let fall her burden, and you may see them still there to this day.

THE ROMANS ARRIVE

BEFORE the start of history, life had continued apparently unchanged for a thousand years or so, here as elsewhere; but once change started it took place at an accelerating rate. Movements of people throughout Europe during the few hundred years before the birth of Christ, caused invasion and aggression which eventually penetrated to the peaceful world of the Conwy Valley. Neither the Stone-Age builders nor their bronze-using successors had apparently needed fortified enclosures. It seems that with the arrival of the Celtic-speaking, iron-using tribes from Europe that state of affairs was over. A new world had started.

We have in the Conwy Valley one of North Wales's best examples of an Iron Age ring fort, the hilltop fortress of Pen-y-Gaer above Llanbedr-y-Cennin (750694). In use probably before and during the Roman occupation, it overlooks the route of the Romans were to take accross the valley and round the slopes of Tal-y-Fan to Bwlch-y-ddeufaen. Its site is impressively well-chosen as a natural defensive outlook, and thus incidentally gives us today an unequalled view of the layout of the lower valley. Below, the pattern of fields and lanes, the farms sheltered in hollows and the clusters of village houses shows us, now, an anciently inhabited and densely-used land. Then no doubt it still retained its element of danger, beyond the clearings and the spreading

8 Pen-y-Gaer hillfort.

9 Fortifications at Pen-y-Gaer hillfort.

10,11 'Chevaux de Frise' at Pen-y-Gaer.

area of worked land. Looking the other way we can still get the feeling of being in isolated and precarious safety bordered by wilderness. That way the upland moors stretch expansively into the heart of the Carnedd mountain range.

The hillfort of Pen-y-Gaer consists of two concentric lengths of defensive wall, one made of stone and an outer one of earth, which may perhaps represent two separate periods of construction. They are most prominent on the gentler southern slopes, and do not occur on the sheer drop to the north, where any potential invader would have had real difficulty approaching. A large broad summit is enclosed by these ramparts, and within it may be seen occasional remains of hut circles. There is certainly room for a very large group of people to take refuge here, and the existence of a similar fort not far away on the coast, on Conwy Mountain, indicates that this area was fairly highly populated when the Romans came.

One remarkable feature of Pen-y-Gaer hillfort, which in fact makes it unique in England and Wales, is the primitive form of tank trap which defends the main approach to its entrance. An area of spiked stones set upright in the ground on this western slope would, when there were presumably more of them, have made it hard to approach at any speed. This rare feature is now known by the French term 'chevaux de Frise', a 17th century cavalry tactic called after the country of Friesland, where it was first used.

Other groups of hut circles similar to those on Pen-y-Gaer can be found in the valley and on its slopes, though some are hard to identify. And in the uplands near Llyn Dulyn (708666), a long scattered settlement stretches along the bank of the stream. In this case the huts and compounds are so similar in form to the Bronze Age settlements on Dartmoor that their use may well date from that earlier age. From Bronze Age times right through to the early Middle Ages the form of dwelling remained the same, a circular foundation of embedded stones rising to a few feet, forming a base from which a wooden superstructure rose to a peak, wigwam-fashion, to be covered with thatch or turf. Only the stone base, of course, remains for us to see where our early predecessors actually lived.

The Celtic Iron Age peoples instinctively defended hilltops, to which they could retreat and from which they could attack. The Roman army operated on a more extended system, of regional headquarters and a chain of auxiliary forts, in which the line of communication was all-important. In this area we have examples of the two crucial ingredients of this system, the Roman road and a fort protective of a river crossing.

The line of the road across the valley floor itself has never been identified, but up on the slope of Tal-y-Fan, where it runs past Maen-y-

12 Aerial photograph of Caerhun Roman fort, called Canovium.

13 Roman road by Bwlch-y-ddeufaen; inset: paving stones on the Roman road.

Bardd, through the pass of Bwlch-y-ddeufaen, and on its way down to the other coast, it can be clearly seen. Sunk into cutting to give a level gradient, paved with small stones throughout its length, it represents, as so many Roman works do, an achievement of impressive thoroughness and care.

They launched their first attack into North Wales under the leadership of Suetonius Paulinus, from the legionary headquarters at Chester, in the year 61 A.D. It is likely that the road across the hills originates from that expedition, and that a small field fort would have been established in the valley. Their purpose was to invade and subdue the island of Anglesey, which, Tacitus tells us, 'was feeding the native resistance'. This first invasion however met with failure. With the Roman general and a large part of the army so far away, the Britons of the south-east, under their famous queen Boudicca, took the opportunity to revolt. Suetonius had hardly reached Anglesey when the news came, and the army in Wales had to withdraw at once and set out on that effective system of routes on the long march south.

It is probable that the more substantial fort at the river crossing dates from the second, more extended, campaign. In the late summer of A.D. 77 the tribe whose territory was North Wales, known to the Romans as the Ordovices, ambushed and massacred, somewhere near our area, an outpost of Roman cavalry. This was a serious blow to Roman morale, and demanded action.

The new Roman governor of Britain, Agricola, took the courageous decision of marching into North Wales late in the year, risking a winter campaign in the mountains. He pursued the Ordovices, perhaps taken off-guard, into their strongholds, and 'cut to pieces', Tacitus says, 'almost the whole fighting force of the nation.' To consolidate this victory he decided to carry through the earlier abortive attempt to occupy Anglesey.

One of the key elements in a strategy involving moving men between Chester and Anglesey was the protection of the crossing of the Conwy river, particularly as this point could also be supplied by sea. The crossing place which the Romans chose was a little upstream of later ferries and bridges, and would no doubt have been the junction of the lowest possible fording point with the highest navigable tidal water at that time. It lies at Caerhun, near to the present church and hall of that name. (776703).

Although the site has been fully excavated, the ground was filled in and covered over again afterwards, and not much can be seen now except the mounds and banks which show the lines of its walls. A few pieces of walling remain revealed among the tree roots, and from some of these one can see that the Romans imported Cheshire sandstone. Agricola's first fort would have been made of wood and earth, and any visible remains must belong to the stone-built expansion of the early second century A.D.

ORIAICIACIT
CARAVSIV
HICIACIT
INHOCCO
CERIESLA
PIDVM

THE ROMANS ARRIVE

Finds indicate that the fort remained in use until the early 120's, when troops were removed from many parts of Britain to help in the construction of Hadrian's Wall. After that, its use declined, and archeology indicates that by about 180 A.D. it was no longer occupied.

Part of the explanation for this Roman presence on the bank of the Conwy may possibly be the importance to Rome of British pearls. A Latin historian records that Julius Caesar himself was impressed by their size. It is known that Conwy's pearl industry, which took place up the river until modern times, was extremely ancient. The pearls grew in the large fresh-water 'horse-mussels', which some people claim may still be found in the Trefriw area.

Whatever the reason for their coming and remaining, there is no doubt that the effect of it was to put North Wales on the map. The existence of that road set the pattern for future communications, and facilitated movement into and out of the area from then on. The existence of that Roman community at Caerhun gave an impetus to a settlement pattern within the valley, and no doubt stimulated activity which helped to stir the valley from its long sleep.

LLYWELYN FAWR

THOUGH the early stirrings in the valley bottom no doubt set the long-term pattern for the future, it was rather in the valleys of its headwaters and upper reaches that life around the river Conwy began to develop towards modern times. Through Dolwyddelan the Lledr river, a notable stream in its own right, runs to lose its identity in the Conwy above Betws-y-Coed; the substantial tributary of the Machno flows through the village of Penmchno to join the Conwy a little higher up; and the infant river itself, rising in Llyn Conwy on an undistinguished moor (780460), passes through an attractive small-scale valley in which lies the village of Ysbyty Ifan.

It is in these upper reaches that the first signs of modern life took shape, and one of its earliest symptoms was the coming of Christianity. This seems to have arrived here early, judging by the discovery in and around Penmachno churchyard of five early Christian tombstones.. One of them contains a reference which dates it fairly certainly to A.D. 540; another, which must be similar in date, has the early-Christian monogram known as Chi-Rho,

14 **Early Christian tombstones at Penmachno church.**

15 Ysbyty Ifan bridge.

16 The old church at Llanrhychwyn.

from the Greek letters XP, the first two letters of the word Christos, which are put together to form a cross with a rounded head. This stone refers to the person whose tomb it marks as lying 'in hoc congeries lapidum', *'in this heap of stones'*, indicating perhaps that the ancient Bronze Age custom of building a cairn over a tomb survived into Christian times in these remote places.

Christianity clearly also took root in the neighbouring valley of the upper Conwy, since the name of Ysbyty Ifan, *John's Hospital*, refers to an importance which this place had quite out of proportion to its size and quietness today.

Towards the end of the 1180's the Knights of St. John of Jerusalem established a hospice for travellers crossing these otherwise inhosp-itable moors. One wonders why, and the explanation probably lies in the great holiness of Bardsey Island, off the Gwynedd coast, which became a place of pilgrimage. Pilgrim routes were inevitably punctuated by such hospices as that founded at Ysbyty.

There is nothing to see of this foundation now, but a visit to the church will reveal the surprising continued importance of this religious site into history. Some alabaster effigies, unfortunately now in a poor state, commemorate one of the area's great families. Rhys ap Meredith lies there, beside his wife and son. He was Henry Tudor's standard bearer at the Battle of Bosworth, and was felled by Richard III himself, seeking his rival. The son who lies beside him here at Ysbyty, now sadly headless but visibly dressed in ecclesiastical robes, became chaplain and cross-bearer to Cardinal Wolsey.

The right of sanctuary which had been provided by the Knights of St. John when founding their hospice, was extended by Llywelyn Fawr, *Llywelyn the Great,* to include most of the upper Conwy, and the hospice rose to prominence as a famous centre of hospitality during the Middle Ages. This role degenerated in the 15th century, however, when the immunity from the King's laws which went with the right of sanctuary was abused to the extent of making Ysbyty a refuge for lawbreakers.

To Llywelyn, however, the religious aspect was no doubt paramount. He consistently used his great power in support of the church. Though he became effectively Prince of all Wales, his place of origin and the area of his deepest concern was the valley of the Conwy and its uplands.

Beyond Dolwyddelan there stands a fortress which might have been designed for romantic effect as well as for defence (722523). A single sturdy tower remains, rising firmly from its crag against a usually stormy sky. This is a truly Welsh castle, built by the independent princes long before the English wars began.

The family of the ancient kings of Gwynedd, the rulers who

17 Maenan Abbey remains.

18 The stone base of Llywelyn's coffin, in the Wynn chapel.

took over control of the area when the Romans left, had remained in control of it during the Middle Ages. It was one of their descendants, Iorwerth, son of Owain Gwynedd, who built Dolwyddelan castle in 1170. His son Llywelyn, who came to be known to history as Llywelyn Fawr, was therefore very probably born there.

Llywelyn rose to power during the 1190's, and by the end of the century he was the ruler of all of Gwynedd. He proved to be a wise and capable politician, and it was during his period of dominance that Wales came nearest to achieving that elusive independence and unity which it has always felt to be its right. England under King John was unstable and vulnerable, and Llywelyn astutely used his powerful neighbour's precarious state to exploit Wales's new unity. As acknowledged leader of the Welsh chieftains he succeeded in ridding Wales of the Norman power with which it had been gradually infiltrated.

The Conwy Valley has the honour of having close connections with this great statesman. Llywelyn is said to have built himself a residence – probably a hunting court – at Trefriw, in the heart of the valley, where tradition claims that he founded the parish church. Before that was built, it is said, he and his wife Joan (the natural daughter of King John) used to walk up the steep track to the older church of Llanrhychwyn (774616). Legend says he built the church in the valley to save his wife the effort of this walk.

Anyone coming up to Llanrhychwyn today enters at once that pure ancient world of the Middle Ages in which Llywelyn lived. The building is squat, sturdy and simple, shelterd by magnificent yews. The country around is upland farmland, at the point at which the valley slopes break into a plateau of mountain pasture, the tree-line fragmenting, the sky broadening, the air sharpening with mountain freshness. 'The old church of Llywelyn', as it is sometimes called, still in occasional use, is in character with this terrain.

The oldest part, perhaps built in the 12th century, is the wall and neighbouring corner around the doorway. The font ahead of the entry is probably also of this date. The church was lengthened and the chancel added probably in the 15th century, and the north aisle added in the early 16th. Another ancient mountain church may be seen above Henryd, that of Llangelynnin (751737). Here too a simple medieval building (now the western nave) was extended by the addition of the present chancel in the 15th century.

Llywelyn was a devotedly religious man, and among the historic acts for which he found time was the foundation of the Abbey of Aberconwy, the first settlement where Conwy now stands, to which he gave a charter in 1189. No doubt he was a frequent visitor to the monastery there,

19 The old screen now in Llanrwst church.

20 Old engraving of Llanrwst church.

and it is appropriate that it was there that he died and was buried, in the year 1240.

The relative stability which Llywelyn had achieved was not to last, and the war between his grandson, Llywelyn ap Gruffudd, and King John's grandson, Edward I, culminated in a massive invasion of North Wales in 1282. Dolwyddelan castle, which the last prince had made his headquarters, fell to the English in January 1283, enabling Edward to march down the western side of the Conwy Valley and control the crossing place at Conwy.

In order to build his famous garrison town there, the king first had to move the occupants, the monks of Llywelyn's Cistercian Abbey. He gave them new territory in the valley, and transported the monastery wholesale to Maenan (789658) where it remained until the Dissolution of the Monasteries. Very little may be seen of it there now, only a few foundation stones in the grounds of the Maenan Abbey Hotel. The monks took with them, however, the coffin of their patron, enclosed in a magnificent stone sarcophagus. After the Dissolution this disappeared, and only the rediscovered bottom half of the stone casing may now be seen, housed in the Wynn chapel at the old church of Llanrwst (798616), in which church is also preserved the Abbey's magnificently carved rood-screen. It is not known where is the final resting-place of the remains of Llywelyn Fawr.

21 Old print of Dolwyddelan castle.

THE WYNNS OF GWYDIR

THERE is something in the style of the Wynn chapel at Llanrwst which contrasts with its parent body, that sound medieval parish church. It has a flare, an air of confident distinction. The explanation is simple: it is a true product of the Renaissance.

The effects of a new national attitude under the Tudor monarchy were not slow to reach North Wales, where a well-established local aristocracy lacked only the opportunity to take part in English affairs. When this was granted by the Act of Union of 1536, families such as the Wynns, who were already great and powerful locally, were quick to export their ability and enterprise to London.

The chapel was built as a memorial to the greatness of the family by Sir Richard Wynn, the second baronet, in 1633. It is possible that Inigo Jones, then at the height of his career as a fashionable architect, who is thought to have had local connections and perhaps to have been a friend of the Wynn family, had a hand in its design. There is, however, unfortunately no certain evidence for this persistent tradition.

One cannot move in Llanrwst or its area without being aware of the influence of the Wynns. To get to the church by the river, for instance, you pass a line of almhouses which were founded by Sir John Wynn, the first baronet, to house twelve old men of the parish. Their simple elegance proclaims their period. It was in general a time of high quality.

To get a feeling of the power and stability of the Wynns one has to go to Gwydir itself, their family seat. The family was descended from the kings of Gwynedd, by a parallel line to that of Llywelyn Fawr. They bought the Gwydir estate from Llywelyn's great-grandson at the end of the 15th century. The Wynn family had originated in south-west Gwynedd, from where they moved to occupy Dolwyddelan castle in 1488. After the purchase of the estate the great-grandfather of the first baronet built the house at Gwydir.

It is a fine example of a Tudor country house, now unfortunately smaller by one wing than that occupied by Sir John, but still in good condition. It sits securely among protecting trees, one of which was planted to commemorate the wedding of Charles I. The interior contains some fine ceilings and panelling, and some of the windows and doorways appear to have been made from stone dressed for another purpose, presumably therefore retrieved from the demolished abbey at Maenan.

22 Gwydir, inset showing the old courtyard.

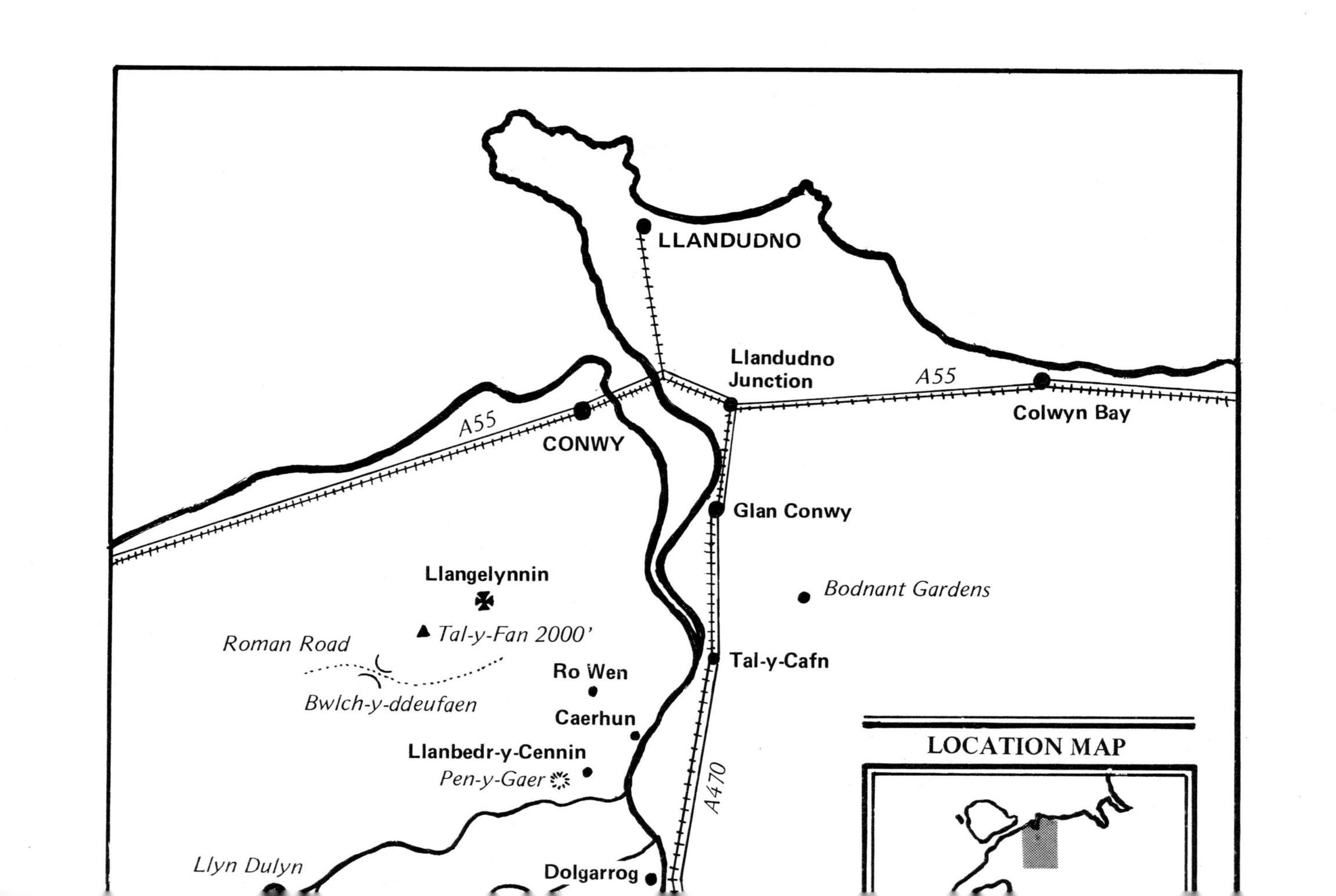
LLANDUDNO
Llandudno Junction
A55
Colwyn Bay
A55
CONWY
Glan Conwy
Llangelynnin
Bodnant Gardens
Tal-y-Fan 2000'
Roman Road
Tal-y-Cafn
Ro Wen
Bwlch-y-ddeufaen
Caerhun
Llanbedr-y-Cennin
Pen-y-Gaer
A470
LOCATION MAP
Llyn Dulyn
Dolgarrog

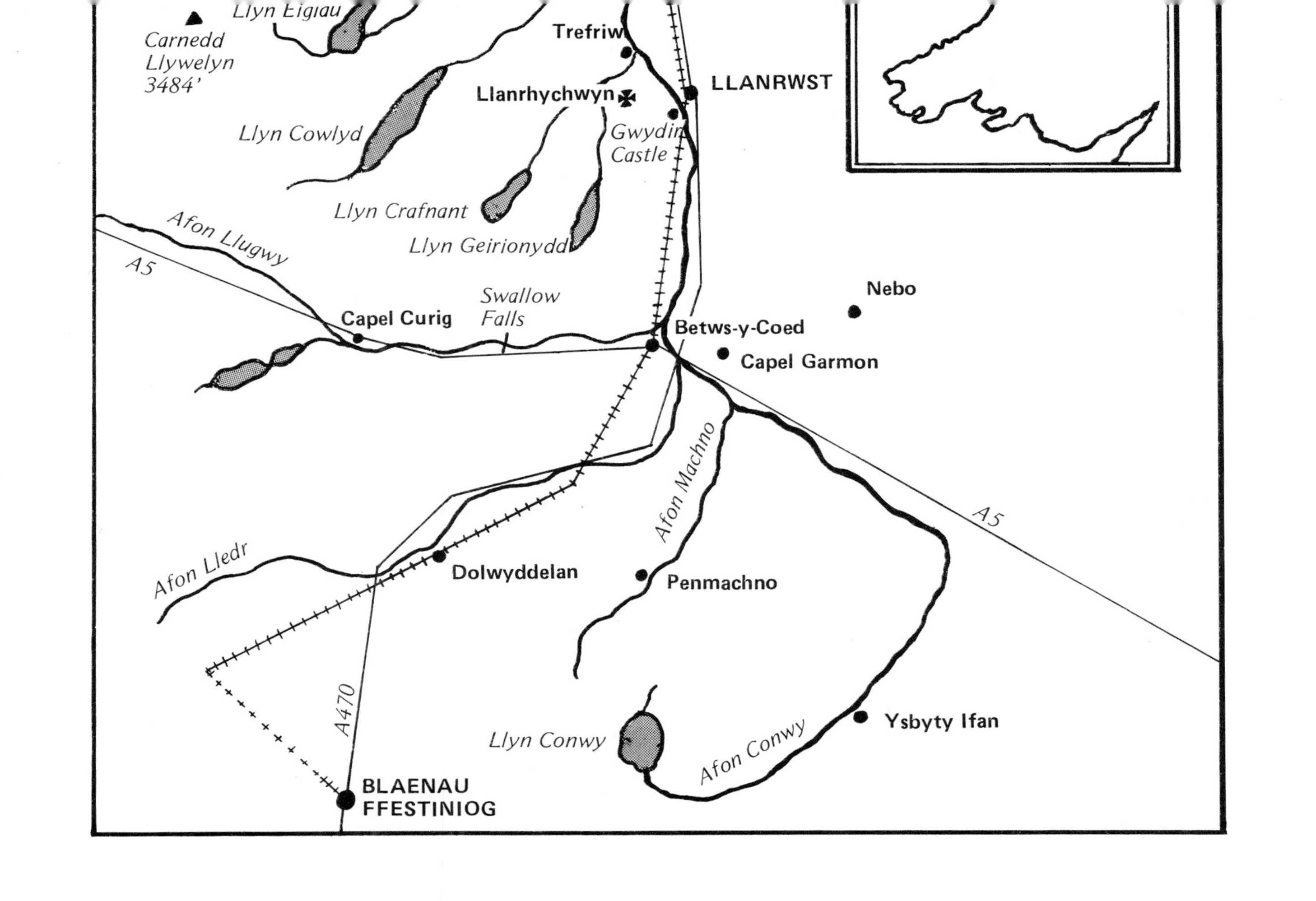
Llyn Eigiau
Carnedd Llywelyn 3484'
Trefriw
LLANRWST
Llanrhychwyn
Llyn Cowlyd
Gwydir Castle
Llyn Crafnant
Llyn Geirionydd
Afon Llugwy
A5
Swallow Falls
Capel Curig
Betws-y-Coed
Nebo
Capel Garmon
Afon Machno
A5
Afon Lledr
Dolwyddelan
Penmachno
A470
Llyn Conwy
Afon Conwy
Ysbyty Ifan
BLAENAU FFESTINIOG

25 Llanrwst bridge and Tu-Hwnt-i'r-Bont.

24 Llanrwst market in the 1930's.

THE WYNNS OF GWYDIR

The family history of the Wynns was written by its most notable member, Sir John, who was among other things a competent historian. The reputation of the first baronet, however, is not otherwise as impeccable as would be appropriate to the high position of his family. Sir John was ruthless in his exploitation of tenants, to the extent that legal cases were brought against him by his more humane neighbours. Threatened with arrest, he used his family's connections at court to buy himself a pardon. His energetic pursuit of wealth enlarged the Wynn estate, and incidentally improved the Conwy Valley. The mining of lead above Gwydir, workings of which can still be seen on the road up to Llyn Geirionydd, was one of the enterprises started by this powerful man. He improved the course of the Conwy itself in order to bring boats up to Gwydir, and actively encouraged local industries such as weaving and fishing. But in the end tradition is unforgiving, and his soul is said to be condemned to remain, trapped for ever, under the Swallow Falls waterfall at Betws-y-Coed.

25 Engraved portrait of Sir John Wynn.

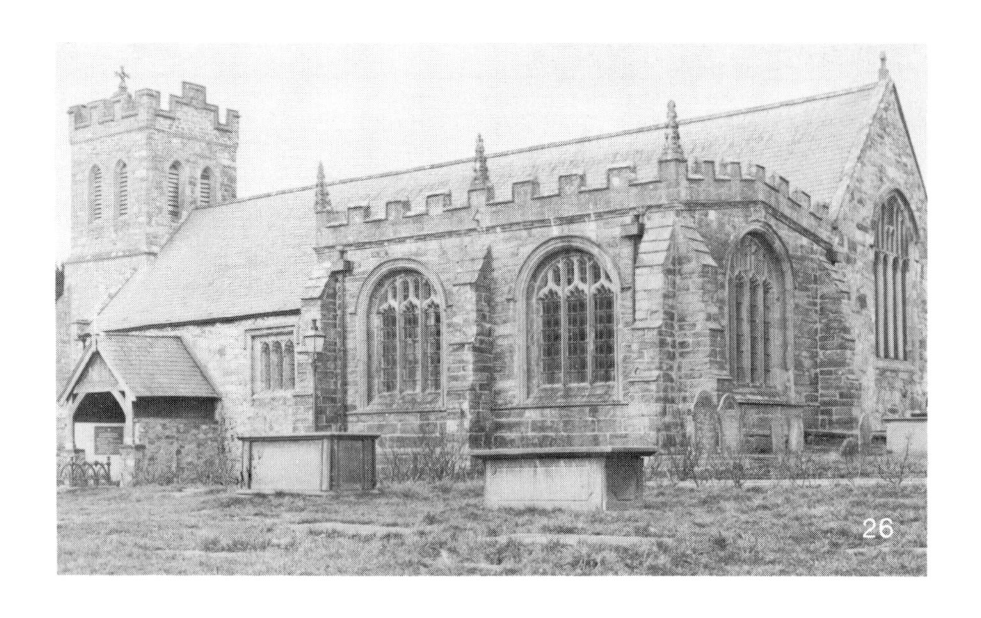

26 Llanrwst church, showing Wynn chapel.

27 Wynn memorial in the chapel.

28 The almshouses near the parish church.

When he died in 1627, at the age of 73, his son Richard inherited the estate and title. While still the heir Sir Richard had risen to prominence at the court in London, and was among the party which set out to Spain in 1623 to arrange for the marriage between Prince Charles, the future Charles I, and the Princess Henrietta Maria. Fortunately for later historians the Wynns were great letter writers, and we have an intimate view both of these great events and of the day to day life of the time:

> *Westminster. Sir Richard Wynn to his father Sir John at Gwydir. Is safely arrived after a long and tedious journey, and is in good health. The Prince is not yet come. Castile and Aragon together are not worth one of the worst counties in Wales. The Welsh mountains are but mole-hills, but their barrenness is most fruitful in comparison with Spain. Henceforth the writer will believe everything reported of another country rather than go to see it.*

Throughout these remarkable times Gwydir continued to receive news from its representatives in the greater world. The Civil War, the Restoration, the plague and the fire of London all get reported by the sons of Gwydir writing home.

When Sir Richard built the Wynn chapel to commemorate the times of greatness he ensured the success of his aim by the quality of work contained in it. The chapel is a treasurehouse of commemorative art. The engraved portraits of members of the family, including the great Sir John, convey an impressively detailed record of the styles of the time, as well as of the strong features of the Wynns. Near the base of the coffin of Llywelyn Fawr lies a stone figure of great stature, dressed in full armour of the 14th century. This is Hywel Goch, a natural son of David, Prince of Wales, who distinguished himself at the battle of Poitiers. On the other side of the room a large stone slab commemorating the sons of John Wynn bears the words 'Funus, Fumus, Fuimus, Ecce', a cryptic Latin motto – literally, *'death, smoke, we have been, behold'* –which may perhaps suggest to different people different shades of interpretation. Wooden rails at either side of the chapel bear strangely primitive carved heads, the work no doubt of a local craftsman of both talent and independence of mind.

The same sort of freedom from convention is apparent in another Wynn chapel, also built by Sir Richard (in 1673), that of Gwydir Uchaf, up the hill above the main house. This was a private family place of worship, built in connection with the upper mansion, which the Wynns used in preference to the larger and older house below during much of the 17th century.

29 Interior of Gwydir Uchaf showing the painted ceiling.

30 Gwydir Uchaf.

31 Old doorway, showing date, at Gwydir Uchaf.

The chapel's most remarkable feature, one in fact which makes it a national rarity, is its imaginatively painted ceilings.

The paintings show angels taking part in the fundamental Biblical scenes of creation, revelation and judgement. In contrast to the conventional nature of the themes, however, the style is free of all received notions of correctness, the whole approach being audacious and individual to the point of idiosyncrasy. As a result the work is notable for its energy and simplicity, transmitting a freshness and directness which a trained or educated artist could never have achieved. Sir Richard had been Treasurer to the Queen's Household, and as such no doubt saw such things as the work which Inigo Jones was carrying out for Henrietta Maria at Greenwich. He had travelled abroad, and was indeed in a position to import artists from anywhere to complete his chapel. In commissioning, as it seems evident that he did, a local artist of enterprise and ability, did he foresee the extraordinary effecitveness of this result? What, one wonders, was his reaction to the finished work? Did he appreciate its clarity and honesty, as we do? For once the Wynn papers are strangely silent.

Although Llanrwst is particularly fortunate to possess all these features, its most conspicuous feature is inevitably its bridge, the 'Pont Fawr' still splendidly in use in the late 20th century despite its great age. Its predecessor had fallen into 'the greatest decay' by the 1620's, and the two counties which it joined, Denbighshire and Caernarvonshire, between them raised the £1,000 necessary for its replacement, which was constructed in 1636. The legend that Inigo Jones designed it (along with the Wynn chapel) is so persistent as not to be ignored, and there is no doubt that Sir Richard would have had plenty of chance to get to know the great architect. Possibly he did a sketch for it while staying at Gwydir; but it must be said that there is no evidence, and the fact that the record of its origin – the demand for a new bridge, the raising of the money, and so on – makes no mention of this distinguished connection, rather indicates that it arose at a later date.

The bridge is steep enough now, but in early prints its slopes are even more precipitous, and it is known from the records that it was modified in the 1670's (when the central arch had collapsed) and again in 1702.

Since there was no other crossing place in the valley until the 19th century, the existence of this bridge made Llanrwst the hub of communications. As movement increased during the 17th and 18th centuries this factor became more important. An old house at one end of the bridge, Tu-hwnt-i'r-bont, *'beyond the bridge',* which dates from the 17th century, and an old inn, Pen-y-bont, *'head of the bridge',* at the other, show how the town formed at an early date around the river crossing. Llanrwst contains even today more than its share of well-established hostelries, and in early coaching times there would have been very many more.

HAFOD AND HENDRE

THE history of land-use in the Conwy Valley is a matter of the development of natural resources, and the most important of these was of course the land itself. Forest clearance probably started to make an impact on the valley slopes in the fifth or sixth centuries. From the occupation of cleared land in the form of round-hut settlements and associated field systems, there developed the medieval farmsteads centred on the long hut, a transition from the ancient hut circle to the modern farmhouse. These, where it has been possible to date them, seem to belong to the 14th and 15th centuries.

It was from those in turn that the upland farm developed, and during the succeeding centuries right up to our own an effective system of co-operation between the hills and the valley arose, the double use of the 'hafod' and the 'hendre'. This involved a system known to geography as seasonal transhumance, the movement of stock from valley to hill land in the spring, and back to the valley for the winter. It is a practice which still in effect continues today, but in the age of landrovers and tractors it is possible to work the two farms from the greater comfort of the valley. The crucial difference is that previously the whole family went too, and the result must have been a shift of population counterparting the great movement of flocks which we can still see taking place.

The hafod, the *'summer dwelling',* was the seasonally-inhabited upland fram which now no longer exists. Many of them stand in ruins on the tracks up to the lakes of Crafnant, Cowlyd and Eigiau. Although the habit of wholesale transhumance declined during the last century, and it is probably more than a hundred years now since any family made the seasonal movement to the hafod in the spring and back to the hendre, *'the old homestead',* for the harvest, several of the old hafod farms remained in occupation by sheepfarmers within living memory.

The fact that it has been actively and continuously farmed is largely responsible for the present appearance of the landscape. The valleys a maze of hedged fields, the upland slopes kept bare of scrub by the persistent browsing of sheep; and everywhere that feature so characteristic of Welsh landscape, the great dry-stone walls, stretching across the mountains for mile after mile.

32 Ruins of a hafod below the Eigiau Valley.

33 Penmachno mill.

34 Trefriw mill.

35 Ysbyty Ifan mill.

These strongly-built structures arose during the last century in connection both with the seasonal use of valley and hill, and with the mixed farming of both sheep and cattle. The 'mountain wall' along the contour limits the height below which the sheep are brought in the winter and the cattle permanently contained. The walls climbing the ridges, on the other hand, are mainly the boundaries of property. They are not essentially intended to prevent the straying of flocks, since the mountain sheep are quite capable of scaling them, and since this is anyway effected by another means. The sheep of this area have an inbred tendency to remain on the 'cynefin', the pasture which goes with the farm and on which they were reared. This conditioning is passed from ewe to lamb generation after generation, and it means that if a mountain farm changes hands the flock must pass with it.

Not only the farming traditions but the stock itself are part of a very old-established system. The original local breeds of both sheep and cattle still predominate in the valley's farms. They are hardy and economic, and permit the efficient use of otherwise marginal land. The Welsh Black cattle, probably among Britain's oldest breeds, are fine sturdy animals, with long curved horns. The Welsh mountain sheep as exemplified here are also probably an original British breed, ideally adapted to this terrain. They are small but compact and well-fleshed, agile and sure-footed, with exceptionally thick fleeces. The rams are decorated with magnificent curved horns.

That, the farming of cattle and mountain sheep, is the valley's oldest and most enduring industry. It gave rise to several effects at an early date which continue to influence the valley life. The development of Llanrwst into the substantial agricultural centre which it now is, and has been for generations, was perhaps one of the most prominent of these. At first a point of travel, it is now essentially the valley's market town. Of great importance to the other valley settlements also was the use of one of the area's products, the treating and working of wool.

From the beginning, wool had been turned into cloth on the spot, rather than exported in its raw form. Until the start of the last century this was largely a cottage industry, but from the early 1800's the idea of centralising the process at a village mill began to take root in North Wales. In our area, a water-powered woollen-mill occurred first at Penmachno, in the second decade of the 19th century, where the mill still forms a prominent part of the village. And in the heart of the valley at Trefriw the business of cloth weaving became a major industry, and has remained so to the present day. The fine, substantial woollen-mill there now is a successor to generations of mills at Trefriw, which was evidently a milling centre even before it became a cloth-weaving one, as far back as the 14th century. The typical Welsh weave produced there from the fleeces of local mountain sheep is superior in quality to its early predecessors,

36 Quarry above Eigiau Valley
37 Ruins of Eigiau slate works.
38 Old mine chimney at Nant-Bwlch-yr-Heyrn
39 The working mill at Glan Conwy

but retains the warmth and durability to which they owed their success.

The use of water-power enabled this product of agricultural enterprises to become an industry. It was, of course, not an invention for this purpose but an imitation of something already taking place, since corn had been ground by water-power for centuries. An old corn-mill with its wheel still in place may be seen on the upper Conwy at Ysbyty Ifan, and in this case the old use of water-power was adapted to modern times by the fitting of a turbine in the 1930's, by means of which it supplied the whole village with electricity until the early 1960's. Down the valley, at Glan Conwy, a 17th century corn mill has been painstakingly restored, and is now once again in the business of producing flour from grain.

This enterprising little business is open to the public during the summer season, and is not just fascinatingly instructive about the way water-power works; there is also something deeply satisfying about the rhythms of falling water and turning wheels, the slow regular pulse of the combined splash, creak, thump and rumble.

40 The present-day cattle market at Llanrwst.

TRADE AND TRAVEL

DURING the 19th century the world was changing fast, and the increase of industry and urbanisation in the English Midlands had a crucial impact on North Wales. One essential element of this expansion was a vast demand for roofing slates, and it happened that among our natural resources was a plentiful supply of suitable stone.

The great quarries developed further up in the mountains, at Llanberis, Bethesda and Blaenau Ffestiniog, but the pressure was such that even these foothills around the valley were searched for suitable outcrops. During the 1820's quarries developed in Cwm Eigiau, above the valley, and around its tributary above Penmachno. It was quarrying also which gave rise to a substantial village on the Lledr at Dolwyddelan. A miniature rail-track took the slates down from Eigiau to the river, where a wharf with a crane loaded it onto boats. Slates from the contemporary quarries at Penmachno also came down the valley to make use of the crane here to be loaded for shipment. The demand gradually slackened and smaller quarries such as these became unprofitable, and ceased to work, during the 1870's, although the works at Penmachno continued to operate remarkably up to the 1950's.

For a time however the area's exports increased: flour, grain, wool, cloth, slate, timber from the Gwydir forests, minerals from the mines above Trefriw and Llanrwst, and a large supply of bark which was used for tanning. With so much produce converging into the valley, the navigable Conwy river became a useful waterway, and a quay developed at Trefriw which remained in use into modern times. Until the second World War a regular paddle-steamer service used to ply between Trefriw and Conwy.

Lower down the Conwy, meanwhile, a port had developed at Glan Conwy, to serve the Denbighshire bank and the lower valley. Here larger vessels – of up to forty tons – received the goods brought down by carters and housed there in several large warehouses. The last of these great sheds, a fine sturdy building probably of the 18th century, may still be seen beside the road. Until Thomas Telford in effect dammed the river to achieve his Conwy crossing, in 1826, the channel was deeper and unsilted on this eastern bank.

The ships taking the valley's produce out from the Glan Conwy bank would of course bring the valley's supplies in, and goods from Dublin, Liverpool and Chester arrived at these old warehouses for distribution to the villages.

41 Pont Gethin, carrying the Conwy Valley railway line accross the Lledr Valley between Betws-y-Coed and Dolwyddelan.

42 Trefriw wharf, showing the old river steamers.

43 Tal-y-Cafn before the bridge.

Before Telford built the causeway the lower Conwy was not bridged. Anyone wishing to cross downstream of Llanrwst would have to go by ferry. There are records of a ferry at Tal-y-Cafn as early as the 14th century, and since the bridge there was not opened until 1897, a great deal of traffic must have passed by that means during the centuries of expansion of trade and travel. The road along the coast via Conwy was in general more convenient, but the dangers and delays of the ferry there were so great that many travellers found it necessary to go up to Tal-y-Cafn and over the route of the Roman road through Bwlch-y-ddeufaen. Richard Fenton, writing as late as 1813, is typical of many reports:

> *we waited in vain for two hours for the ferry boat, the wind being too high to admit of its crossing, which obliged us to go all round to Tal-y-Cafn; and then, through a most tempestuous night over Bwlch-y-ddeufaen to Aber.*

No doubt the inn at the ferry (which still goes by that name) owes its ultimate origins to these times, when the growth of the cities of Liverpool and Dublin, and trade between them, made it necessary for more people to travel this route. It is mentioned several times in the 19th century, in connection with the ferry. Some evidence that this was a well-used coach route arises in the name of a ruin perched above the old road near Pont Hafodty-Gwyn, 'White Hart' (736706), which seems likely to have provided refreshment for travellers, before, or after, the undertaking of the mountain

44 An old warehouse at Glan Conwy.

45 Betws-y-Coed.

46 Waterloo Bridge at Betws-y-Coed.

crossing. At the foot of this route, 'The Old Bull', still very much in use, served the same purpose, while lower still, 'Y Bedol' *(The Horseshoe)* indicates by its name its connection with both coach travel and droving.

The records show in fact that this route very nearly became the main road to Anglesey and Ireland, a circumstance which would have radically affected the settlement pattern of North Wales. The Caernarvon Turnpike Trust obtained an Act of Parliament in 1777 enabling it to build a new road along this route, but they never succeeded in raising the necessary money. Had they done so then perhaps Telford's bridge at Conwy would not have been considered necessary, and without his causeway there the railway might have gone through North Wales much further south, with the further result that there would have been no resort towns of Llandudno and Colwyn Bay.

As it is Tal-y-Cafn is now rural and peaceful, and the congestion of the modern world crosses the Conwy valley by one or other of Telford's two routes, the A55 through Conwy, or the A5 which shortly preceded it through Betws-y-Coed. This passes over the river on a fine cast-iron bridge, known, from its opening date of 1815, as the Waterloo Bridge.

Though the ferry at Tal-y-Cafn drew much less unfavourable comment than its counterpart at Conwy, it was still operating seventy years after the lower estuary had been bridged, in a time which expected better facilities, and it was with great relief that local people greeted the 'Tal-y-Cafn Bridge Act' of 1894, and attended the eventual opening on 9th October, 1897.

The Shrewsbury to Holyhead road had passed through the mountains since the late 18th century, when Lord Penrhyn improved the pass of Nant Ffrancon, and by the early 19th century it had become a mail route. Thomas Telford was commissioned in 1811 to survey the whole matter of the road from London to Holyhead, and one of his solutions was to make use of the existing route from Shrewsbury through Llangollen to the Conwy Valley (which of course was obliged to run via Llanrwst in order to cross) by joining it up with Lord Penrhyn's turnpike by a more direct route.

Hence we have now the old-established travellers' posting-point of Betws-y-Coed. It was built to cater for the needs of visitors, which it still most effectively does. A number of old inns which served the Victorians on tour still provide a suitably substantial air of welcome. A battery of shops retail both high-quality local produce, and lesser knick-knacks which holiday-makers are apparently thought to wish to take home as mementoes. The congestion to which all this gives rise at the height of the season renders Betws-y-Coed temporarily unbearable. But either side of this period its unchallengably attractive setting, on another of the Conwy's main tributary rivers, the Llugwy, coupled with the air of well-established substance which it owes to its history, makes it a place which well deserves its fame and popularity.

47 Trefriw Spa, renovated and reopened recently.

48 The Bodnant Gardens

TRADE AND TRAVEL

Travel for its own sake, and for the enjoyment of the scenery, was largely a 19th century innovation, pioneered as far as North Wales is concerned by writers such as Pennant and George Borrow. From the start the valley was ready to provide facilities, and the spa at Trefriw (its waters still flowing, though at present little used) was a flourishing and fashionable centre of relaxation when watering-places were in vogue.

Travel, moreover, was boosted and facilitated by a new means of transport at this time. During the 1860's the branch line from Llandudno Junction was developed, completed to Betws-y-Coed by 1868. It still provides by far the best way of viewing the valley's scenery, a journey of great variety and spectacular effect which can stand comparison with the world's more famous rail trips. By this means visitors may now travel through the mountains to Blaenau Ffestiniog, where the Ffestiniog narrow-gauge railway joins up with this line from its long climb up from the other coast, and where too the two slate-quarrying museums of Llechwedd and Gloddfa Ganol offer a fascinating insight into the workings of some of the largest slate-producing undertakings in the world.

Down in the valley, meanwhile, another of our present major attractions was taking shape. In 1875 Mr. Henry Pochin chose a valley near Eglwysbach in which to found his ideal garden, and Bodnant Gardens now display in their full maturity the realisation of his plans. The soil and climate of this secluded spot favour the spring shrubs for which the gardens are rightly famous, and they are best seen as early as possible in the open season.

History does not stop. We are making it ourselves; and a complex world such as that of the Conwy Valley continues to develop, to change, and in some ways to improve. It remains, however, firmly and very healthily agricultural, still centred on its market town, Llanrwst.

Only at Dolgarrog, perhaps, has the industrial age made any noticeable impact on the rural landscape. The aluminium works there provides valuable opportunities of employment in an area where that otherwise is a constant problem. Dolgarrog is unusual too for being the site of tragedy; in November 1925 a dam which had been constructed to turn the lake at Eigiau into a reservoir leaked causing a breach to occur in a lower reservoir and releasing a torrent which destroyed much of the village, including the church. Fortunately it was the night of the weekly picture show, and most of the children were in the village cinema, which was clear of the course of the flood. Sixteen of the villagers lost their lives in the disaster.

Alongside the agricultural activities which are so much part of its long history, the valley now maintains its tradition of providing for visitors. Hotels such as the Waterloo and the Gwydir at Betws-y-Coed reflect the days of coach travel along Telford's great road, and down in the valley bottom

substantial country houses have become hotels at Maenan, where both the Maenan Abbey and the Plas Maenan offer accommodation in pleasant surroundings.

The villages of the west side, Llanbedr and Rowen, in the meantime, have retained their intimacy and peaceful character in spite of a substantial change in population, since this is an area much sought after by those who move to North Wales to live. While down at the valley's mouth Glan Conwy has almost ceased to be a village at all, rather approaching the size of a small town, so much building has now been permitted there.

Though undoubtedly much of the present which the long past has created, and the surviving elements of that past themselves, can best be seen by using a car, there are aspects of the valley which are better seen by other means. There is no substitute for footwork in the hills. But the size and space and lie of the land can be fully grasped only from the river itself, and fortunately regular trips from Conwy quay make the journey of the navigable tidal water during the summer months.

This river view, together with the valley branch line (which one hopes will survive to become as widely appreciated as it deserves to be) helps to give an overall impression of the Conwy Valley's form and nature. Bearing in mind at the same time the considerable richness of its past, one comes to recognise it as a place of very strong identity.

49 Trefriw, and a view of the valley.

50 The Conwy Valley Railway Museum at Betws-y-Coed.

A BRIEF INDEX